Fabric Crafts

Fabric Crafts

A handy step-by-step guide

DK

LONDON, NEW YORK, MELBOURNE,
MUNICH, DELHI

Project Editor Katharine Goddard
Senior Art Editor Elaine Hewson
Managing Editor Penny Smith
Senior Managing Art Editor Marianne Markham
Producer, Pre-Production Rebecca Fallowfield
Senior Producer Katherine Whyte
Special Sales Creative Project Manager Alison Donovan

DK INDIA
Editors Janashree Singha, Manasvi Vohra
Senior Art Editor Balwant Singh
Art Editor Zaurin Thoidingjam
Assistant Art Editor Nikita Sodhi
DTP Designer Satish Chandra Gaur

First published in Great Britain in 2014
by Dorling Kindersley Limited
80 Strand, London WC2R 0RL

Material in this publication was previously published in:
Craft (2012)

A Penguin Random House Company

Copyright © 2012, 2014
Dorling Kindersley Limited

2 4 6 8 10 9 7 5 3 1
001 – 188230 – Jun/2014

This edition produced for The Book People Ltd,
Hall Wood Avenue, Haydock, St Helens, WA11 9UL

A CIP catalogue record for this book is available
from the British Library

ISBN 978-1-4093-6972-1

Printed and bound in China by Leo Paper Products Ltd.

Discover more at **www.dk.com/crafts**

Contents

Introduction

DIP-DYEING • TIE-DYEING • FABRIC MARBLING • FABRIC PAINTING

BLOCK PRINTING • SILKSCREENING • FABRIC STENCILLING

BATIK • PATCHWORK • APPLIQUÉ • BEAD EMBROIDERY

Fabric is a wonderful way to add colour, texture, and interest to your home and your wardrobe. Fabric crafts embrace a wide range of diverse disciplines, from dyeing and decorating to stitching, weaving, and felting, so there are plenty of methods here to inspire you.

This book shows you simple ways to make decorative and practical items using fabric for your home – as well as one-off items of clothing. There are a number of ways to decorate and manipulate fabric and fibres without using specialist equipment or expensive materials and, once you've familiarized yourself with the techniques, there's plenty of scope to apply your own creativity. Discover how exciting it can be to dunk fabric into a dye bath and see it emerge, transformed into a kaleidoscope of colour. Find out how you can apply fabric paints in a variety of ways to a number of different items, such as a plain cook's apron or tea towel. A length of fabric can be decorated with eye-catching motifs then, with some simple stitching – no complicated sewing skills are required – made into a shoe bag, cushion cover, or sarong.

Patchwork and appliqué are popular crafts and you need only the most basic sewing skills – and a sewing machine – to make an heirloom bedspread or a cosy throw. A dazzling choice of fabrics is available to buy in the shops or online – though if you're already a seasoned stitcher, you will no doubt have suitable scraps of fabrics lurking in a drawer or work basket, destined to be joined together to make a pretty patchwork. While you have your sewing machine at the ready, try your hand at ribbon weaving, or if you prefer hand-sewing, embellish a plain cardigan with beads.

The pages on silkscreening and batik provide an introduction to crafts that you might have thought were too complex to attempt, but the illustrated techniques and step-by-step projects demystify the processes involved, allowing you to try out these crafts for yourself.

Tools and materials

Crafting with fabrics allows you to really put your creativity to the test: immerse yourself in the colours, textures, and patterns that fabrics have to offer. You'll probably already have most of the tools and materials listed here. A sewing machine comes in handy for larger projects, but is not a must.

Dip-dyeing and tie-dyeing

Measuring jug This is essential for measuring both dry ingredients such as salt, and wet ingredients like water. A glass jug is less likely to become stained with dye than a plastic one.

Plastic container A medium-size or large plastic tub is useful for immersing fabric in dye solution and is a better option than using the kitchen sink, which might become stained.

Fabrics Choose 100% cotton, linen, or silk. Wash in hot soapy water and rinse before dyeing to remove any dressing.

Rubber bands and string Both of these are useful for tying fabric prior to dyeing to create patterned effects.

Dyes Cold water dyes are suitable for dyeing natural fabrics such as cotton, linen, and silk. Mix the powder according to the instructions on the packet.

Fabric marbling

Cotton fabric White cotton absorbs dye best. Aim for 100% cotton and avoid polycotton mixes as the dyes will not adhere to them successfully.

Marbling dyes These dyes come in a variety of colours with a pipette or dropper for easy application. Use two or three colours at a time for best results.

Marbling combs and stylus These tools are used on the floating dye to achieve a variety of marbled effects. If you can't get hold of a marbling comb, use an ordinary wide-toothed comb instead.

Marbling size Usually sold as a powder, it is added to water to create a jelly-like base on which to drop marbling dyes, so that they float on the surface.

Plastic tray This needs to be wide enough to accommodate the fabric when it is laid out flat.

Fabric painting

Fabric paint pens Use these to outline edges and define shapes once the main design is complete.

Dressmaker's carbon paper Allows you to transfer designs onto your chosen fabric. If the lines are too faint, go over them with a pencil.

Fabric paints These are available in a wide range of colours that can be mixed to create your own shades.

Artist's paintbrushes You'll need good-quality paintbrushes in a range of sizes to add colour and detail to designs.

Block printing

Fabric paints Specially formulated fabric paints come in small jars. Colours are intermixable and can usually be "fixed" onto fabric by pressing with a hot iron – check the instructions on the garment's label.

Wooden blocks These provide a firm base for homemade printing blocks. Children's wooden building bricks are ideal.

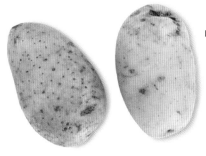

Potatoes The cut surface of a potato provides an excellent surface for printing. Large potatoes are best, as they are easy to cut and hold.

Craft foam This foam rubber, available in small sheets, can be cut with scissors or a craft knife and is used to create block printing shapes.

9

Silkscreening

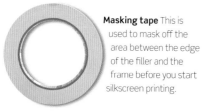

Masking tape This is used to mask off the area between the edge of the filler and the frame before you start silkscreen printing.

Old toothbrush Helps remove drawing fluid from the mesh of the frame.

Drawing fluid This special ink is used for "drawing" the design onto the mesh of the frame.

Screen filler This specialist product is applied once the drawing fluid is dry to mask out the areas you do not wish to print.

Silkscreen printing frame with mesh The frame should be large enough to contain the image, with some room to spare around it. Some frames are hinged but you don't need a hinged frame when printing on fabric.

Fine paintbrushes You'll need a selection of good-quality fine paintbrushes.

Squeegee Use a squeegee or plastic spreader to apply the screen filler and silkscreening inks to the mesh.

Fabric screen printing inks These are special paints for silkscreen printing on fabric.

Fabric stencilling

Cardboard A piece of cardboard is useful to protect the work surface and absorb excess paint.

Stencil brushes These short, stubby brushes are used specifically for stencilling. Make sure you have a selection of sizes.

Freezer paper This special paper is coated with plastic on one side and is used for creating stencils. Make sure you buy freezer paper and not wax paper, which is coated on both sides.

Fabric paints These are special paints for use on fabric. Use them as they come or mix to achieve the desired colour.

Batik

Cold batik wax This is a water-based wax that can be used cold and is suitable for beginners. Stir well before using.

Wax-Out liquid This emulsifying liquid is diluted with warm water and used to remove wax from the completed piece of batik.

Tjanting This has a metal reservoir with a spout affixed to a wooden handle and is used to apply lines of wax. They come in various sizes.

Brushes You'll need several brushes. Chinese calligraphy brushes make great wax brushes. A foam brush, or a sponge, is useful for applying wax to larger areas of fabric.

Patchwork

Patchwork ruler This wide see-through ruler has precise markings for measuring strips, squares, and other geometric shapes. It is used in conjunction with a rotary cutter.

Waddings Waddings are usually either wool, cotton, or polyester. Wool and cotton shrink, so wash them before using.

Cutting shears Used for cutting large pieces of fabric, the length of the blade can vary from 20 to 30cm (8 to 12in).

Rotary cutter This tool has a circular blade that rotates as the cutter is pushed or pulled across the fabric. It can be used freehand but is designed to be used against the edge of a patchwork ruler.

Appliqué

Bonding web This web of special glue on a paper backing is ironed onto the back of appliqué fabric to enable the appliqué to be bonded in place.

Decorations Buttons, beads, and sequins are just some of the decorations you can use to embellish any appliqué project. If using beads or other decorations on washable items, make sure they are colourfast.

Bead embroidery

Embroidery hoop This is used to keep fabric taut while working embroidery or other forms of needlework. Embroidery hoops are made of wood, plastic, or metal.

Water spray This is useful for removing traces of water-soluble pen.

Water-soluble pen A water-soluble pen looks like an ordinary felt-tip pen but the ink disappears when sprayed or dabbed with water. It is useful for tracing or marking designs on fabric.

Dip-dyeing TECHNIQUES

The most straightforward dip-dyeing techniques involve natural fabrics – cotton, linen, and silk – with dyes that can be mixed using hot tap water. Dyeing fabrics produces attractive results, so try your hand at dyeing household linens such as sheets and pillowcases, or clothing such as T-shirts and socks. For best results when using new fabrics, wash first to remove the "dressing" in the fabric as this will prevent the dye from penetrating the fibres.

Preparing the dye bath

dissolve salt in hot water

1 Always read the dye manufacturer's instructions. For dyes that require the addition of salt, dissolve the salt in very hot tap water.

dissolve dye in water

2 Dissolve the sachet of dye powder in the specified amount of water, stirring until dissolved. For large amounts of fabric, you may need more than one sachet.

3 Combine the salt solution and the dye in a large plastic tub. Top up with enough water to cover the fabric, following the instructions on the packet.

Dyeing fabric

1 If the item is new, wash it to remove all traces of dressing, otherwise, just wet it. Place the damp item in the prepared dye solution, making sure it is completely submerged.

2 Move the fabric in the dye from time to time. It's best to use a metal or plastic spoon, or an old wooden spoon, as the wood will become permanently stained with dye.

3 After the specified time, remove the item from the dye bath, handling it with rubber gloves to prevent your hands from staining. Rinse thoroughly in cold water, then wash with hot water and detergent.

Dip-dyeing

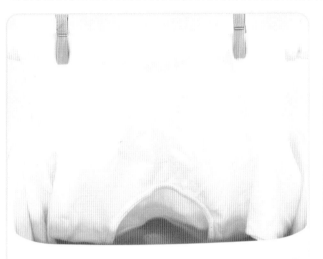

1 Instead of dyeing an item one colour all over, submerge only part of it in the dye. Suspend the item by rolling it around a stick, such as a bamboo pole, and hold it in place with pegs. Rest the pole on the rim of the tub. If you allow the fabric to drape over the side of the tub, the dye will seep up into the damp fabric.

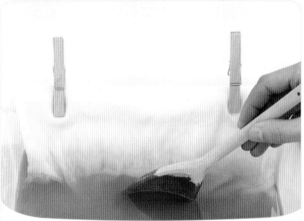

2 Stir the dye from time to time, carefully moving the fabric as you do so to ensure an even result. After the specified time, rinse in cold water until the water runs clear.

3 If you wish, you can mix up a second colour and dip the undyed portion in this dye. Again, suspend the item over the dye bath, keeping the part you do not wish to dye clear of the sides of the tub.

4 By carefully choosing colour combinations, you can create some interesting effects. Here, yellow and red dyes have been used. On one T-shirt the dyes have been allowed to overlap slightly, while on the other, an undyed band between the two has been left.

Dip-dyed café curtain PROJECT

With just one sachet of dye you can create subtle colour effects – perfect for a café curtain. If you're dyeing an existing curtain with a dye suitable for natural fabrics, check the fibre content of your curtain before embarking on the dyeing process. Alternatively, you can make your own curtain from cotton muslin. Make sure you stitch it with 100% cotton thread so that both the fabric and the thread take up the colour.

YOU WILL NEED

- cotton curtain
- fabric detergent
- bamboo, wooden, or plastic pole
- measuring jug
- salt, if needed (check instructions on dye packet)
- cold-water fabric dye
- plastic tub or other suitable container
- rubber gloves
- metal, plastic, or old wooden spoon

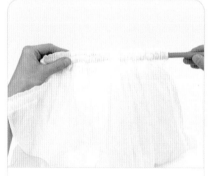

1 Wash the curtain and leave it damp. Slip a pole into the casing at the top of the curtain.

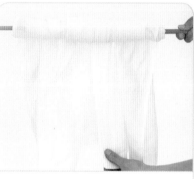

2 Roll the fabric around the pole, leaving the bottom section – about a quarter of the total length of the curtain – free.

3 Prepare the dye according to the manufacturer's instructions and pour it in the tub. Wearing rubber gloves, submerge the bottom section of the curtain in the dye bath for 20 minutes, resting the pole across the rim of the tub. Stir the dye gently from time to time to ensure even coverage.

4 After 20 minutes, unroll another length of the curtain so that about one-third is submerged in the dye. Soak for a further 20 minutes, then unroll a little more, so that about three-quarters of the curtain is in the dye. Soak for a further 20 minutes.

5 Remove the curtain from the dye and remove the pole. Rinse the curtain thoroughly in cold water, then wash in hot water and detergent, following the manufacturer's instructions. Iron before hanging.

Tie-dyeing TECHNIQUES

Tie-dyeing is an easy method of creating colourful patterns on clothing and home furnishings. For best results, use pure cotton fabrics and cold-water dyes. There are some tried-and-tested techniques of folding and tying the fabric to produce patterns such as circles and stripes. If you decide to use more than one colour, dye the lighter colour first.

Choosing items to dye

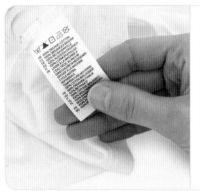

Check the label on the garment: for cold-water dyeing, choose items that are 100% cotton, linen, or silk. Wash the fabric first in hot water and detergent to remove the dressing.

Preparing the dye bath

Mix the dye according to the manufacturer's instructions and pour it into a container large enough to hold the fabric being dyed.

Creating a striped effect

1 To create a striped pattern, place the fabric on a flat work surface. Starting at one edge, pleat the fabric into concertina folds.

2 Bind the pleated fabric tightly using lengths of string. Bind at intervals along the concertina folds.

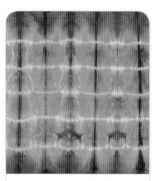

3 Submerge the fabric in the dye (in this case, deep pink) for the recommended time, stirring occasionally and keeping the fabric submerged. Remove from the dye, rinse in cold water until the water runs clear, then remove the strings.

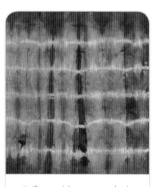

4 If you wish, you can pleat and bind the fabric again, and dye it a second colour. In this case blue was used, creating purple patches where the blue dye has overdyed the pink stripes.

Creating large and small circle motifs

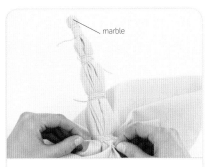

marble

1 For a large circle motif, place a marble in the centre of the fabric and bind around the base with string to hold it in place. Pull the fabric into a cone shape with the marble at its tip, then bind at intervals.

2 For smaller circle motifs, tie single marbles tightly into the fabric using lengths of string. Submerge the fabric in the dye bath for the recommended time.

3 Remove the fabric from the dye and rinse thoroughly in cold water, then remove the strings and marbles. When the fabric is opened out, you will see the large and small circle motifs.

Creating a multicoloured swirl effect

1 Place the fabric on a flat work surface, pinch the centre, and twist it in a circular motion to form a spiral.

2 Secure the twisted fabric tightly with two rubber bands crossing in the centre and dividing the fabric into four sections.

3 Mix up dye in two or more colours – here, four different colours have been used. Instead of submerging the fabric in the dye, use a paintbrush to apply a different colour to each section. Apply the dye liberally and push it into the folds. Wear rubber gloves to avoid staining your fingers.

4 Place the dyed fabric in a plastic bag, seal, and leave for 24 hours (or according to the manufacturer's instructions), then rinse thoroughly in cold water and remove the rubber bands to reveal a colourful swirl pattern.

Tie-dyed T-shirt PROJECT

Choose a T-shirt that is 100% cotton. (Note that if the thread used to stitch the garment is made from synthetic fibres, it will not absorb the dye and will retain its original colour.) Wash the T-shirt before dyeing and leave it damp. The T-shirt shown here has been dyed using pink and purple; you could choose your own combination of colours, bearing in mind that, where colours overlap, they'll produce a third colour. For example, yellow and blue overlapping will make green.

YOU WILL NEED

- plain white cotton T-shirt
- string
- scissors
- measuring jug
- cold-water fabric dyes in pink and purple
- plastic tub or other suitable container
- rubber gloves
- metal, plastic, or old wooden spoon
- detergent

centre front of T-shirt

1 Find the centre front of the T-shirt and pull it up to form a cone shape. Starting at the tip of the cone, bind it at intervals with lengths of string. Bind the top of each sleeve in the same way.

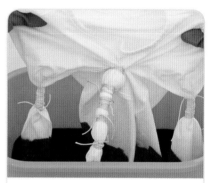

2 Prepare the pink dye and pour it into the tub, adding enough cold water to completely cover the garment. Wearing rubber gloves, submerge the T-shirt in the dye bath. Stir from time to time.

3 After 1 hour (or the recommended time), remove the T-shirt from the dye and rinse it in cold water until the water runs clear. Remove the strings. Discard the pink dye.

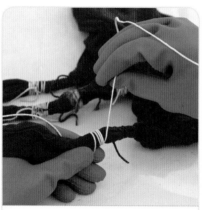

4 Repeat Step 1 to bind the front and the top of each sleeve again. Where the new strings are tied, the underlying colour will remain, so tie some strings around the white areas and some around the pink areas.

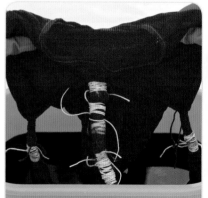

5 Prepare the purple dye and pour it into the tub, adding enough cold water to completely cover the garment. Submerge the T-shirt in the dye bath. After 1 hour, remove and rinse thoroughly in cold water.

6 Remove the strings and wash the T-shirt in hot water and detergent to fix the dye.

Fabric marbling TECHNIQUES

Fabric marbling requires patience and can get messy, so always make sure your work surfaces are properly protected. You'll need to experiment with various tools and colours before you settle on a pattern you like. Look at the end papers of old books to give you inspiration for a design.

Preparing the bath

Follow the manufacturer's instructions to make a marbling bath. Dissolve 1 teaspoon of "size" in 1 litre (1¾pt) cold water in a large plastic tub and stir well. For best results, leave to set overnight or for at least two hours before using.

Skimming the surface of the bath

As the bath has been left to settle, you'll need to break the tension on the surface. Do this by skimming the surface with newspaper scrunched into a ball. You'll also need to do this every time you apply fresh dyes.

Adding colour and creating patterns

1 Add a few drops of marbling dye on the surface of the bath so that it is completely covered with dye, then skim the surface with scrunched newspaper.

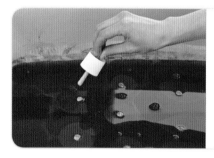

2 Add more drops of the first colour again to cover the surface, then dot a second colour onto the surface in a regular or random arrangement.

3 To create swirls, draw a marbling comb across the surface, from one edge of the tray to the other, pulling the dyes to create a wavy marbled effect.

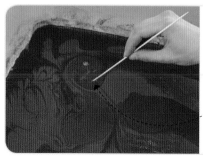

4 Use a stylus, the end of a paintbrush, or other pointed implement to manipulate the colours and create individual swirls.

Experimenting with patterns

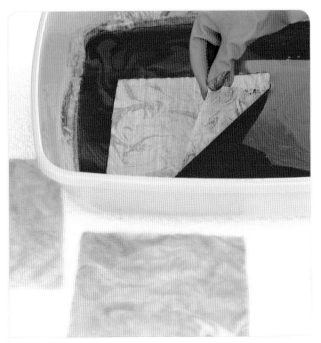

The bath solution improves the more you use it, so view your first few attempts as experiments. Always pre-wash the cotton fabric to make it more absorbent and practise with remnants of fabric, adding more dyes, skimming, and then printing to get an understanding of the patterns that can be created. Always wear rubber gloves to protect your hands from staining.

Marbling the fabric

1 Once you're happy with the marbled effect, lay the fabric onto the surface in one go, patting it gently to ensure there are no creases. Do not move the fabric as this will spoil the pattern.

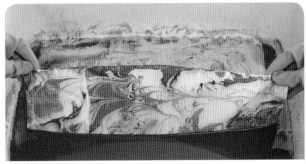

2 Holding on to two corners, lift the fabric up swiftly, holding it over the tub to allow excess water and ink to drip off.

Fixing the colour

1 Leave the fabric to dry face up flat on a towel. Don't hang it up or wash it at this stage as the colours may run.

2 When the fabric is dry, it will be stiff due to the residue from the bath. Rinse under cold running water, then hang up to dry.

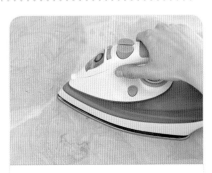

3 To fix the colour, iron the fabric on a medium setting. The fabric can now be washed.

Marbled napkins PROJECT

The unpredictability of marbling is what makes it such a fun craft. Each time you manipulate the dyes, new patterns emerge. If you don't like the pattern, simply skim off the dyes with newspaper and start again. If you like what you see, you can capture it on fabric forever. This introduction to fabric marbling shows you how to create a set of swirling marbled napkins.

YOU WILL NEED

- large shallow plastic tub
- measuring jug
- teaspoon
- marbling size
- newspaper
- blue and green marbling dyes
- marbling comb
- stylus or similar pointed implement
- rubber gloves
- 4 pre-washed white cotton napkins
- old towel
- iron

1 Make a marbling bath by dissolving 1 teaspoon of size in 1 litre (1¾pt) cold water in a tub. Leave to set overnight or for at least two hours. Skim the surface with a ball of newspaper to break the tension.

2 Dot a few drops of blue dye evenly across the surface of the bath. Skim the surface with newspaper before adding more blue dye. Then add a few drops of green dye in between the blue blocks of colour.

3 Draw a marbling comb across the surface of the bath, using a swift movement. If you want a more complex pattern, repeat the movement or use the stylus to create more swirls.

4 Wearing rubber gloves to protect your hands, carefully lower a napkin onto the surface of the bath. Pat it down gently then swiftly remove it. Repeat for the other napkins, skimming the bath and adding more dye each time.

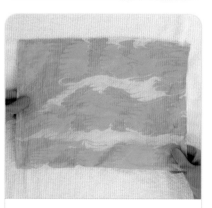

5 Leave the napkins to dry face up flat on a towel, then rinse under cold running water. Hang up to dry, then iron on a medium setting to fix the dyes.

Fabric painting TECHNIQUES

Fabric paints are a permanent way to colour fabrics. They dry quite hard when applied but soften once the fabric has been washed. They can be mixed to create new shades or used straight from the pot, but it's best not to dilute them as you would water-based paints, as this reduces the pigmentation.

Preparing the fabric

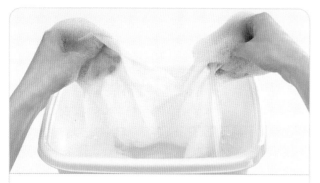

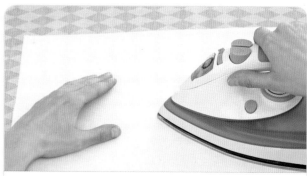

1 Always pre-wash the fabric to make it more absorbent. Rinse and hang up to dry.

2 Once the fabric is dry, iron it to remove any creases. The surface of the fabric should be as smooth as possible, almost like a sheet of paper.

Transferring a template

template with dressmaker's carbon paper underneath

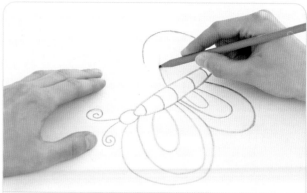

1 Lay a sheet of dressmaker's carbon paper face down on the fabric and secure the template on top. Use a sharp pencil to trace over the template, then remove the carbon paper.

2 If the lines on the fabric are too faint, go over them again with a pencil.

Applying paint

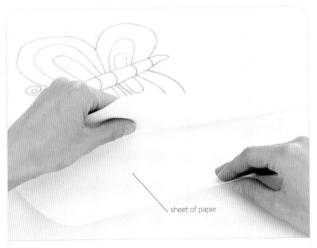

sheet of paper

1 If you're painting onto a double layer of fabric (such as a bag for instance), place a sheet of paper inside the bag to prevent the paint seeping through to the layer underneath.

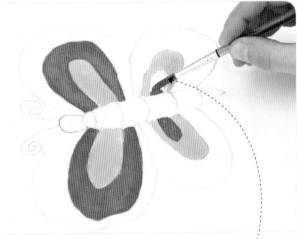

2 Apply the paint in even strokes in one direction. Some colours, especially lighter colours, may require more than one coat. Allow each coat to dry before applying a second.

3 Once the main design is complete and dry, add details with a fine paintbrush or draw on outlines with a fabric paint pen.

Fixing the colour

Leave the paint to dry for 24 hours. Place the fabric face down and iron on a high setting to fix the colours. The fabric can now be washed.

Shoe bag PROJECT

Shoe bags are great for when you're travelling or if you like to store your footwear away neatly. Customize a plain bag by painting on a shoe-themed motif, or draw designs that look like your own shoes, making them easy to identify. Use a mix of fabric paint and fabric paint pens – you can be as intricate as you like or stick to designing with block colours.

YOU WILL NEED

For the drawstring bag

- 1m x 69cm (40 x 27in) pre-washed white cotton
- cutting shears
- dressmaking pins
- sewing machine
- white thread
- 150cm (60in) ribbon
- iron

For the motif

- dressmaker's carbon paper
- pencil
- sheet of paper
- fabric paints
- paintbrushes
- fabric paint pen

1 To make the bag, fold the fabric over by 5cm (2in) along one long side. Pin and tack. Using a straight stitch on the sewing machine, sew along the edge of the fold to create the ribbon casing.

2 Fold the fabric in half lengthways with the casing on the outside. Sew the bottom and side edges using a straight stitch, stopping at the casing using a safety pin. Feed the ribbon through the casing then turn the bag to the right side.

3 Transfer the template on p.56 onto one side of the bag, following **transferring a template** on p.24. Make sure the design is centred.

4 Slip a sheet of paper inside the bag to protect the bottom layer. To prevent the colours merging, allow each colour to dry before painting the next. Add a second coat of paint if required.

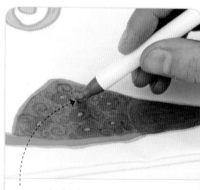

5 Use the fabric paint pen to outline the shoe and draw on the swirls. Leave to dry for 24 hours.

6 Place the bag face down and iron on a high setting to fix the colours.

Block printing TECHNIQUES

Block printing was first practised in the Far East, centuries ago. Wooden blocks were carved with designs, coated with inks, and used to print onto fabric. Using a printing block allows you to make simple repeat patterns on fabric quickly and easily with the minimum of mess. You don't need any special materials to make a block: craft foam and a piece of wood, or even a potato can be used to create simple, eye-catching designs.

Making a foam block

1 Draw your design on a scrap of craft foam. Simple, symmetrical shapes are the most effective and easiest as you don't have to worry about the fact that, when printed, your design comes out reversed.

2 Cut out the shape, using scissors. For a flower centre, as here, also cut away the centre of the flower using a craft knife over a cutting mat.

3 Apply an all-purpose glue to one side of the foam shape and stick the shape to a wooden block, such as a child's building brick.

4 For a more complex motif that is to be printed in different colours, make separate printing blocks for each element – here, the second element is a one-piece leaf and stem.

Printing

3 Add further prints in different colours, as required, to complete the motif.

4 Allow the paint to dry completely, then fix the dye with a hot iron according to the manufacturer's instructions. Place a clean cloth over the fabric to prevent scorching.

1 Apply fabric paint to the entire surface of the motif. If the paint is fairly liquid, use a paintbrush; for thicker, stiffer paint, use a roller. To make sure you're happy with the design, test it on a scrap of fabric before printing a larger piece.

2 To make a print, place the paint-coated motif in position on the fabric and press down firmly, taking care not to move the printing block, or the image will be blurred.

Making a potato stamp

1 Slice a potato neatly in half, making sure the cut surface is level and smooth. Draw the shape onto one half using a felt-tip pen.

2 Cut around the outline of the shape using the tip of a sharp knife, then cut away excess potato around the shape.

3 To add intricate detail to your design, use a knife or lino-cutting tool to gouge out small pieces of potato within the shape.

4 Wipe the surface of the potato with kitchen paper to remove any excess moisture, then apply fabric paint. Press the paint-coated surface firmly onto the fabric, hold for a few seconds, and then remove.

Block-printed apron PROJECT

Decorate a plain apron with simple printed motifs, such as these stylized fish and citrus slices, to make a lovely gift for a cook. You can buy a plain apron or make one yourself. Check the instructions on your fabric paints before you embark on the project: some paints work best on natural fabrics such as cotton or linen. You will probably be advised to wash and iron the fabric before applying the paints.

YOU WILL NEED

- paper
- pencil
- scissors
- craft knife
- cutting mat
- craft foam sheets
- all-purpose glue
- small wooden blocks
- fabric paints in blue, yellow, green, and white
- medium-size paintbrush
- cotton or linen apron
- clean cloth
- iron

1 Trace the templates on p.57 onto paper, or draw your own. Cut out the shapes then place them on a piece of craft foam and draw around the outlines. Cut out each foam shape using scissors or a craft knife.

2 Glue each foam shape to a wooden block. For the fish, leave a gap between the body and the head.

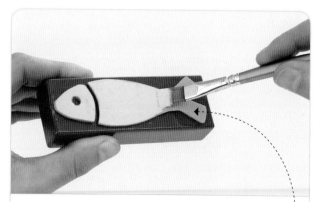

3 Apply fabric paint to the motif using a paintbrush. Most commercial fabric paints are intermixable: if, for example, the blue paint is too strong, you may wish to add a little white to make a paler shade.

4 To print a motif, place the paint-covered block in position on the apron, then press down to make your print. Reapply paint to the block before making second and subsequent prints.

5 Repeat the process to print the other motifs, mixing colours as desired. Leave the paint to dry completely. Place a clean cloth over the printed area, then iron with a hot iron, following the manufacturer's instructions, to fix the dyes.

Silkscreening TECHNIQUES

If you want to print the same image lots of times, either on separate pieces of fabric or on the same piece of fabric, silkscreen printing is ideal. Some silkscreen printing techniques are quite complicated and time-consuming, but this version, using special drawing fluid and screen filler, is a great way to start. You can use it to create reasonably detailed images with a hand-printed feel which you can repeat time and time again.

Applying the image to the screen

Decide on the image you want to use. Here we are using a simple fish shape. Use a pencil to trace the image onto the mesh of the frame. To protect the work surface, place a jar lid underneath each corner of the frame to raise it by about 2cm (³⁄₄in), then go over the lines of your tracing using a fine paintbrush and drawing fluid. Leave to dry.

Applying the screen filler

1 Screen filler masks out the areas you do not want to print. Mix the filler until smooth and spoon it onto the mesh. Using a squeegee, apply a thin, even coat of filler over the screen. Do this in one go – if you try to reapply the filler, you may rub off some of the dried drawing fluid.

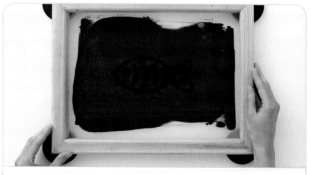

2 Leave the filler to dry in a horizontal position, making sure that the frame is still raised and that nothing touches the mesh while the filler is drying.

3 Once the filler is dry, spray cold water on both sides of the mesh using a shower head or hose fitted to a tap to remove the dried drawing fluid. If any stubborn bits remain, rub gently with an old toothbrush. Leave the filler to dry.

4 Mask any gaps between the edges of the filler and the frame with masking tape on the underside of the frame to avoid unwanted printing ink getting on your fabric.

Printing your fabric

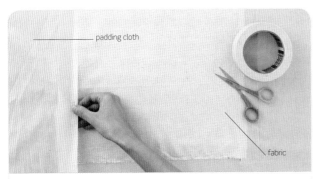

padding cloth

fabric

1 Prepare the work surface by padding it with some cloth such as a smoothly folded old sheet; this will ensure there is good contact between the mesh of the frame and the fabric to be printed. Secure the fabric to the padding cloth using masking tape.

screen filler

printing ink

2 Place the frame in position on the fabric and hold it firmly. Pour about the same quantity of printing ink onto the mesh as the amount of screen filler used.

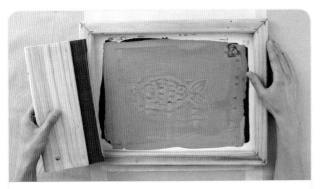

3 Hold the squeegee at a 45° angle and, using reasonable pressure, move it across the image from right to left in one smooth stroke. The image should be well coated with ink. Now pull the squeegee back over the image in the opposite direction.

4 Lift the frame immediately to reveal the silk-screened image. When the ink is dry, detach the printed fabric from the work surface. Place a pressing cloth over the image and, with the iron fairly hot, iron on each side for 3 to 4 minutes to fix the image and make it colourfast.

Silkscreened sarong PROJECT

This spotted cotton fabric has been printed with a classic pattern of a bird perched on a branch in a subtle shade of charcoal grey – a colour produced by mixing standard black and white silkscreen printing inks. The beauty of silkscreen printing is that once your image has been created, you can use it many times over with very little extra effort. To make the sarong longer and give it added appeal, we stitched a colourful border to the two short edges but you could leave it plain.

YOU WILL NEED

- pencil
- silkscreen printing frame
- 4 jar lids
- drawing fluid
- fine paintbrush
- screen filler
- squeegee
- old toothbrush
- masking tape
- scissors
- black and white screen printing inks
- water-soluble pen
- ruler
- 1 x 1.5m (1 x 1.6yd) washed and ironed pale grey polka dot woven cotton fabric
- cloth such as an old sheet
- iron and pressing cloth
- washing up liquid
- nylon scrubbing brush

1 Trace the bird template on p.58 onto the mesh. Raise the frame to protect the work surface. Go over the lines with drawing fluid, filling in the areas shown in grey on the template. Leave the fluid to dry.

2 Apply the screen filler then, once dry, mask the gaps between the edges of the filler and the frame, as explained in **applying the screen filler** on pp.32-33.

3 Mix the black and white inks to make a dark grey, remembering that the final colour will look slightly darker once it has dried.

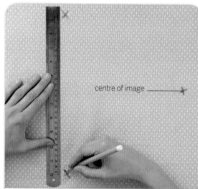

centre of image

4 Using the water-soluble pen, mark the centre of each image, using the picture of the finished sarong as a guide. Each centre should be about 30cm (12in) from the centre of each of the images surrounding it.

5 Print and fix the images as explained in **printing your fabric** on p.33, securing each section you are painting to the padded surface as you go. You'll need to work fairly quickly to make sure that the paint doesn't dry on the mesh and spoil your work. Keep the fabric flat while it is drying so that the wet images do not smudge. Clean your equipment as soon as possible.

Fabric stencilling TECHNIQUES

Stencilling is a really quick and easy way to produce your own bold and quirky designs on fabric and textile items. If you're just starting out, it's sensible to choose a plain, light-coloured fabric and a simple, one-colour design. Once you've learned the basics, you may want to experiment with printing on patterned or darker fabrics, using more intricate images, or building up your image in different layers and using two or more colours.

Cutting and applying a stencil

freezer paper

1 Select the image you want to use for your stencil. For this example, we are using a simple computer-drawn flower head and circle. Cut out a piece of freezer paper that is large enough to leave about 2.5cm (1in) all around the design to make sure that you do not get any paint on the fabric when you come to brush it on.

flower design

2 Place the freezer paper over the design so that the matt (non-glossy) side is uppermost. Trace the design onto the freezer paper using a pencil.

3 Cut out the design carefully, using a craft knife and cutting mat. For the main flower stencil, it is the area surrounding the actual flower head that will form the stencil, so keep this part intact. For the flower centre, you'll need to keep the cut-out circle intact.

4 Position the main stencil and the flower centre onto pressed fabric, making sure the glossy side of the paper is facing downwards. With the iron in the dry mode and on a medium setting, press the stencil onto the fabric, taking particular care to make sure that the edges are well stuck down.

Applying fabric paint

1 Place a sheet of cardboard underneath the fabric. Using a stencil brush, dab the paint over the stencil. Use a small amount of paint at a time and take particular care round the edges. Leave the image to dry thoroughly. If necessary, apply a second coat of paint.

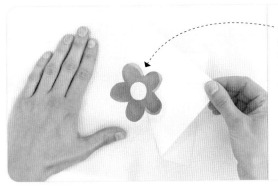

2 Once the image is dry, peel the two pieces of freezer paper away. They should not leave any sticky residue.

Ironing to fix paint

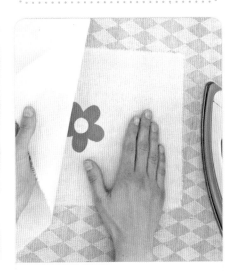

Check the instructions that come with your fabric paints on how to fix the paint. You will normally need to place a pressing cloth over the image and, with the iron set in the dry mode and on the maximum heat for the fabric, iron over the image for one to two minutes.

Masking for second colour and painting

1 To stencil the flower centre in a second colour, cut the flower centre from a piece of freezer paper, leaving a generous frame all round. Position the paper over the flower, aligning the centres.

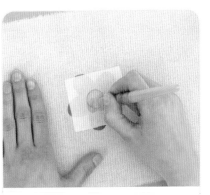

2 Place a sheet of cardboard underneath the fabric and, using the stencil brush, dab the paint over the stencil and leave to dry.

3 Peel away the freezer paper to reveal the finished image and fix the paint, following **ironing to fix paint**, above.

Stencilled tea towel PROJECT

This pure white linen tea towel has become home to six cheerful cups and saucers stencilled in bold shades of red and blue. The basic shape is the same for each teacup but each features different colours and decorations. Choose one of each design as we have done here, or put together your own unique combination. The teacups use only three colours – red, white, and blue – which are mixed to create different shades.

YOU WILL NEED

- 26 x 48cm (10¼ x 19in) piece of freezer paper
- ruler
- scissors
- craft knife
- cutting mat
- hole punch (either single or double-hole)
- plain white cotton tea towel
- fabric paints in bright blue, bright red, and white
- palette
- stencil brushes
- iron and pressing cloth

1 Cut out six cup and saucer stencils from freezer paper using the templates on p.58. Cut out one flower head and one flower centre stencil. Then cut out five stars, one border, four stripes, and one heart (keeping the heart surround as well). Using the hole punch, punch out 15 small freezer paper spots. Arrange the cup and saucer stencils in two even columns on the front of the tea towel and iron them in position. Iron on the stars, spots, flower head, border, stripes, and heart.

2 Use a palette to mix the fabric paints. Using a clean brush for each colour, dab on mid-blue paint to the star cup, bright red to the polka dot cup, bright blue to the flower cup, pale blue to the border cup, and creamy red to the striped and heart cups. Leave the paint to dry.

3 Peel off all the freezer paper. The star and polka dot designs are now complete. The other designs need further stencilling to add the second colours.

4 Place the flower centre stencil in the centre of the flower. For the border and striped designs, use strips of freezer paper to mask off all the areas where you do not want any paint. For the heart design, use the freezer paper from the cut-out heart to mask off the area around the heart.

5 Dab red paint on the flower centre and on the border of the teacup with a border. Dab very pale blue paint on the stripes of the striped teacup. Dab pale pink paint on the heart. Leave to dry, then remove the freezer paper and iron to fix the designs.

Batik TECHNIQUES

Batik is the art of painting fabric using a wax resist. Apply the wax using a paintbrush or tjanting, then paint over the fabric – the waxed areas will repel the paint and retain their base colour. You can use this technique to build up multiple layers of colour and to produce fabulous "crackle" effects. This technique can also be done using a wax pot and hot wax.

Stretching the fabric

Using three-pronged pins, pin all four corners of the fabric to a frame, ensuring the fabric is straight and taut. Next, pin halfway along each side, then pin at regular intervals so that there is a pin every 5 to 7.5cm (2 to 3in).

2 Using a fine paintbrush, paint cold wax over the traced lines: these lines will remain white on the finished piece. Leave to dry naturally for about 20 minutes, or for speed, use a hairdryer on a cool setting.

5 To add further detail, paint a line of cold wax around the inside of the petals. These lines will act as a barrier, keeping the next colour confined to the edges of the petals. Here a tjanting has been used, but you could also use a fine paintbrush.

Painting the design

1 Fix the template under the fabric and trace the design onto the fabric using a vanishing fabric marker pen.

3 Use a medium paintbrush to paint the flower centre and petals with iron-fixed silk paint, right up to the wax lines. Allow paint to dry.

4 Paint the background using a sponge brush dipped in paint. Paint up to the edges of the flower but not over it. Allow to dry.

6 Once the wax has dried, paint between the two wax lines in the petal colour. The second coat will give a darker colour.

Adding crackle

1 Dip a small sponge into cold wax and brush it over the entire surface of the piece. Leave to dry for 20 minutes.

2 Remove the fabric from the frame and scrunch it to crackle the wax. The more you crumple the fabric, the more pronounced the crackle effect will be.

3 Spread the fabric out, face up, on a surface protected with plastic sheeting. Leaving some creases in place, paint over the background using a sponge brush.

4 Wait a few seconds for the colour to sink into the fabric. Darker lines showing on the reverse of the fabric indicate that the crackle effect is working. When you are satisfied with the effect, you can halt the process using a hairdryer on a cool setting.

Setting the paint

Once the fabric is dry, sandwich it between layers of newspaper and iron for three minutes per 30cm (12in) square, keeping the iron moving. This will set the paints and absorb some of the wax. Repeat with clean newspaper until most of the wax has been absorbed.

Removing residual dye and wax

1 Rinse the fabric in cold water to remove the residual dye and more of the wax. Stir 1 tablespoon of Wax-Out liquid into 2 litres (3½ pints) warm (30 to 40°C/ 86 to 104°F) water. Soak the fabric for 10 minutes, stirring gently (or follow the manufacturer's instructions) to remove the remaining wax.

2 Remove the fabric from the Wax-Out solution and wash it gently in hot water with a little detergent. Iron on the reverse while damp.

Cushion cover PROJECT

Batik is a fun way to make a beautiful cushion cover. This project makes one cushion cover with an organic branch and leaf design. Start with plain white cotton and use wax and paints to build up the design in layers. You may wish to paint the back of the cushion to match the front before sewing the back and front together. Make the cover in an envelope-style, or stitch on a zip or buttons.

YOU WILL NEED

- 2 x 45cm (18in) squares of white 100% cotton fabric
- scissors
- 45cm (18in) square wooden frame
- three-pronged pins
- vanishing fabric marker pen
- fine and medium paintbrushes
- cold batik wax
- iron-fixed silk paints in yellow, light green, and dark green
- palette
- water pot
- sponge brush

- plastic sheeting
- small sponge
- Wax-Out liquid
- newspaper
- iron
- detergent

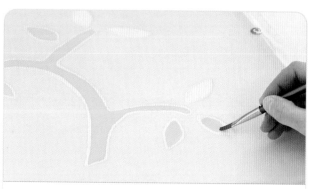

1 Stretch and pin one square of fabric to the frame. Using the vanishing fabric marker pen, enlarge and transfer the template on p.59 to the centre of the fabric. With a fine paintbrush, paint cold wax over the traced lines. Leave to dry for about 20 minutes. Paint the background yellow using a sponge brush, then paint the branch and leaves using light green paint. Leave to dry for 20 minutes.

2 With the template as a guide, paint the lines on the branch and the veins on the leaves. Use cold wax and a fine paintbrush. Leave to dry for 20 minutes.

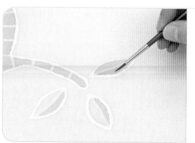

3 Using the dark green, paint alternate stripes on the branch and on half of each leaf. Leave to dry for 20 minutes.

4 Dip a small sponge in cold wax and brush it over the entire piece so that it is covered in a layer of wax. Leave to dry for 20 minutes. Remove the fabric from the frame and scrunch it to crackle the wax. Protect the work surface with plastic sheeting then spread the fabric out, face up. Paint over the yellow background in the dark green, using a sponge brush. Wait a few seconds for the colour to sink into the fabric. When you are satisfied with the effect, use a hairdryer on a cool setting to halt the process.

5 Once the fabric is dry, follow **setting the paint** on p.41. Then rinse the fabric in cold water to remove all traces of dye before soaking in a solution of Wax-Out liquid for 10 minutes. Wash gently in hot soapy water then iron on the reverse while damp. If you wish, you can paint the second square of fabric (the back of the cushion cover) in yellow, then add crackle by using a layer of cold wax and the dark green paint.

Patchwork TECHNIQUES

The secret to successful patchwork is accurate cutting then matching seams carefully before stitching them together. If the seams don't quite match up, try stretching the shorter edge slightly before sewing to ensure accuracy. One of the most important tools for patchwork is an iron; use it on the steam setting when pressing cotton to keep the seams flat and crisp.

Cutting patchwork fabric

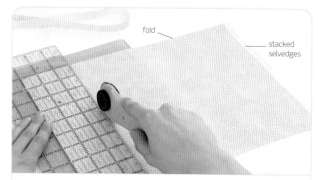

1 Fold a piece of fabric selvedge to selvedge. Press with a steam iron, then place the folded fabric on a cutting mat. Trim the left edge straight, then align a patchwork ruler on the fold so that its right edge is 8cm (3¼in) from the trimmed edge. Cut along the ruler to make a strip. Move the ruler along to cut more strips the same width.

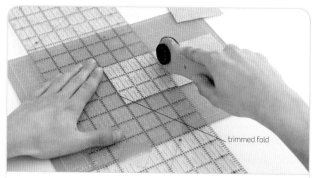

2 Turn the double-layer strip and cut along the fold to make two strips. Using the lines on the ruler as a guide, cut the strips into 8cm (3¼in) squares. If you don't have a rotary cutter, draw pencil lines to mark squares and cut along the lines with dressmaking shears.

Sewing patchwork pieces

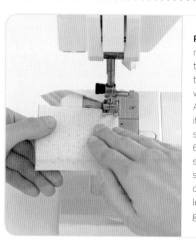

Place two squares with right sides together under the presser foot. Line up the edge of the fabric with the presser foot. Adjust the needle position if necessary to make the seam allowance exactly 6mm (¼in). Stitch the seam. For speed, you can stitch a row of squares one after the other, leaving a small thread gap between them.

Making a complete row

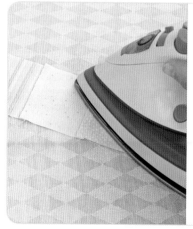

Cut the pairs of squares apart, then stitch one end of a pair to the end of another pair. Repeat this process to make a complete row, then press all seam allowances in the same direction. Press seams in alternate rows the opposite way to reduce bulk when sewing rows together.

Joining rows

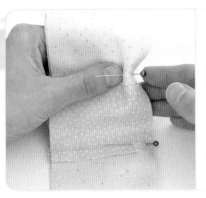

1 Place two rows of squares right sides together. To reduce bulk, ensure the seam allowances in each row face in the opposite directions. Pin together using glass-headed pins and match the seams exactly.

2 Using the edge of the presser foot as a guide, stitch the two rows together, stitching over each pin carefully as you go. Stitch all the rows together then remove the pins. Press all the horizontal seams towards the bottom of the patchwork.

Adding a border

1 Cut two strips the width of the patchwork and twice the depth of the border, plus 12mm (¹⁄₂in). With wrong sides together, press in half lengthways and press one long edge over by 6mm (¹⁄₄in). With right sides together, pin then stitch the unpressed edge to the top of the patchwork. Repeat on the bottom, then press seams outwards.

6mm (¹⁄₄in) turn-over

2 For the long sides, cut two strips the length of the patchwork, plus the top and bottom borders. Press and stitch as in Step 1. Begin stitching 6mm (¹⁄₄in) from the edge and finish 6mm (¹⁄₄in) from the bottom. Repeat on the other side, then press seams outwards.

Adding wadding

1 Cut the wadding and backing fabric to fit exactly between the pressed fold lines in the middle of the border strips. Lay wadding then backing fabric face up on the reverse side of the patchwork.

2 Fold the border along the fold lines at the top and bottom, and pin. Fold the sides to make neat corners. Slip stitch the border to the backing fabric.

Joining the layers

Using strands of embroidery cotton, backstitch through all layers at regular intervals at the intersections. To finish, tie a reef (square) knot at each stitch and trim neatly.

Patchwork bedspread PROJECT

Patchwork is a craft suitable for anyone who can use a sewing machine. This project is ideal if you are new to sewing by machine as all the seams are straight. If you can't find the exact fabrics used here, or wish to change the colour scheme, look for alternative fabrics with the same intensity of colour to achieve a similar overall look.

YOU WILL NEED

- 225cm (2½yd) olive green fabric (115cm/45in) wide
- 175cm (2yd) tiny blue spot fabric (115cm/45in) wide
- 75cm (30in) each of white polka dot fabric and wheel pattern fabric (115cm/45in) wide
- cutting mat
- patchwork ruler
- rotary cutter or dressmaking shears
- sewing machine
- cotton thread in matching colours
- iron
- glass-headed pins
- 145cm x 2m (57 x 79in) thin (2oz) polyester wadding
- 145cm x 2m (57 x 79in) backing fabric
- needle

1 Cut twelve 16cm (6¼in) squares of olive green fabric, 59 squares of tiny blue spot fabric, 22 squares of white polka dot fabric, and 24 squares of wheel pattern fabric.

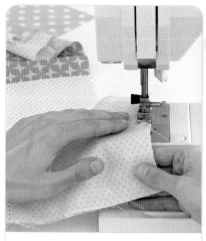

2 Arrange the squares as shown on the diagram on p.60. Following **sewing patchwork pieces** and **making a complete row** on p.44, stitch the squares together in rows.

3 Press the seam allowances on each row to one side. Following the diagram, press the seam allowances on alternate rows in the opposite direction.

4 Pin then stitch the first two rows together, following **joining rows** on p.45. Repeat for the other rows. Press all the horizontal seams towards the bottom of the patchwork.

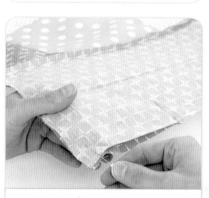

5 Following Step 1 of **adding a border** on p.45, stitch 15cm (6in) wide strips of olive green fabric to the top and bottom of the patchwork panel. Follow Step 2 to attach borders to the sides, then press.

6 Press the whole panel. With the patchwork face down, lay the wadding and backing fabric, face up, on top. Fold the border edges and corners over neatly and slip stitch. Following **joining the layers** on p.45, stitch ties through the layers at regular intervals.

Appliqué TECHNIQUES

Appliqué involves applying fabric shapes to a base fabric and stitching around the shapes. It's a great way of using small pieces of your favourite fabrics to embellish any fabric item. The simplest way to appliqué requires a product called bonding web, which is a thin web of dry glue with a paper backing. Bonding web allows you to create iron-on appliqué shapes very easily. If you are new to appliqué, keep the shapes simple at first before moving on to more complicated creations.

Creating the appliqué

1 Choose the image you want to use for your appliqué and select your fabrics. For this example, we are using a simple hand-drawn owl shape with separate wings. Cut out a piece of bonding web big enough for the owl's body and wings.

2 Place the bonding web over the body and the wings so that the glue side of the bonding web is facing down and the paper side is uppermost. Trace over the images using a pencil.

3 With the iron on a medium setting, iron the pieces of bonding web, glue-side down, onto the reverse of your chosen fabrics. If your fabric has a directional pattern, make sure that the pieces are positioned so that the pattern will be the right way up on the finished shape.

4 Cut out the fabric shapes, paying particular attention around the curves to make sure they are smooth.

Applying the appliqué

1 Peel the backing paper of the bonding web off the owl shape, making sure that the adhesive, now on the fabric, does not stick to itself.

2 Position the body of the owl onto the fabric you are attaching it to and iron it in position.

3 Sew around the shape by hand or with a sewing machine. You can use either a straight stitch or zigzag stitch to do this. If you are using a straight stitch, as shown here, keep your stitching 2 to 3mm (¹/₁₀ to ¹/₈in) in from the edge of the shape.

4 Position and iron the wings in place and sew around them, as explained in Step 3.

Decorating the appliqué

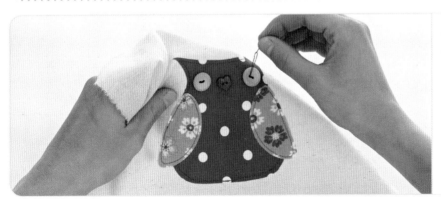

Embellishments such as buttons, sequins, and beads can be sewn on to add interest. Sew on two round buttons for the eyes using contrasting thread. Sew on an orange heart-shaped button for the beak using matching thread.

Appliqué throw PROJECT

A mixture of patterned and plain fabrics has been used to adorn this soft cream-coloured lambswool throw. Of course, you don't have to use the same fabrics that are used here, but when choosing your fabrics, spend time selecting ones that work well together. We have added an assortment of buttons to the flower centres to give the throw a charming homespun look.

YOU WILL NEED

- 4.5m x 50cm (5yd x 20in) bonding web
- pencil
- scissors
- 60 x 150cm (23 x 60in) each of plain light green linen fabric, grey/green floral cotton fabric, and pink floral cotton fabric
- 50 x 70cm (20 x 27½in) each of pale pink cotton fabric and green polka dot fabric
- iron
- 140 x 190cm (55 x 75in) plain cream woollen or fleece throw
- pins
- sewing machine
- cream, olive green, dark grey, and pink sewing threads
- 30 assorted medium-size buttons in grey, cream, red, and green
- sewing needle

bonding web

1 Using the templates on p.61, prepare 15 plain light green base circles, 15 smaller flowers in grey/green floral, 15 outer circles for them in pale pink, and 15 smaller inner circles for them in green polka dot. Then prepare 15 larger flowers in pink floral, 15 outer circles for them in green polka dot, and 15 smaller inner circles for them in pale pink.

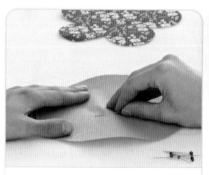

2 Peel away the backing paper of the bonding web and arrange a row of five alternating green circles and pink floral print flowers across the top of the throw, starting with a green circle. Pin them in position. Then arrange the second row, starting with a pink floral print flower. Iron them in position. Repeat these two rows twice more.

3 Sew around the edges of the green circles and pink floral print flowers in straight stitch. Peel away the backing paper on the grey/green flowers and iron them onto the green circles then stitch around these. When sewing the appliqués, keep cream thread in the bobbin and match the top threads to your fabrics.

4 Apply the two centre circles to each flower. Stitch around the pink circles in pink sewing thread and the green polka dot circles in olive green thread, remembering to keep cream thread in the bobbin throughout.

5 To finish, sew a button to each of the flower centres.

Bead embroidery TECHNIQUES

Beading is a great way to breathe new life into clothes and accessories. You can use almost any shape of small- or medium-size beads for beading. Small glass beads known as seed beads or rocailles, and bugle beads, which are small glass tubes, are the most popular and easy to work with. Also, as they are small, they will not weigh your fabric down too much. You can do beading on patterned fabrics to add detail to a pattern or you can create your own beaded motifs.

Preparing the design

1 Decide on the embroidery design and the item you want to embellish. Here we are using a simple hand-drawn flower on fine white linen fabric. Trace the design onto the fabric using a water-soluble pen.

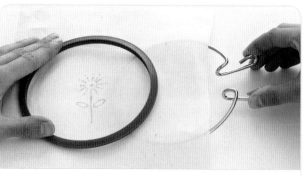

2 Place the fabric in an embroidery hoop and make sure the fabric is taut.

Applying the beads

1 The flower centre consists of a large bead with a small one on top. Using thread that matches the top bead, secure the thread at the flower centre. Take the thread through the large bead, then the small bead, and back down the large bead. Secure it.

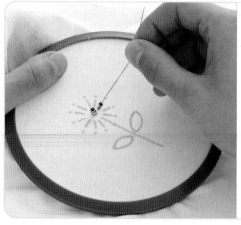

2 To apply beads to the petals, secure a length of pink thread at the inner edge of the first petal. Take the needle through a bugle bead and back into the fabric immediately at the end of the bead. Then take it out again a seed-bead width further on. Thread the seed bead on the needle and backstitch it in place.

3 Thread a second bugle bead on the needle and take the needle into the fabric at the end of the bead. Make a backstitch through all three beads, from the inner to the outer edge of the petal.

4 To apply the outer seed beads, use white thread so you can take the thread between the beads on the reverse of the fabric. Secure the first bead with two backstitches, then take the thread down and along the reverse of the fabric to the position of the next outer seed bead.

Stitching a line of beads

1 To make the stalk, secure green thread at the starting point. Thread four green seed beads onto the thread and take the thread down into the fabric just by the end of the last bead. (If you take it too near the starting point, the beads will not lie flat; if you take it too far away, the row of beads will be too slack.) Take the thread out to the front again, two beads back. Then take the thread forwards through those two beads.

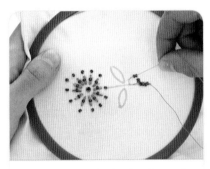

2 Pick up another four beads on the needle and repeat Step 1 until the line of the stalk is complete. Secure the thread.

Filling an area with beads

1 Outline the leaves using the same techniques as for the stalk, but curving the line slightly as you go. Work two short rows of seed beads within the outline to fill.

2 Work a number of virtually invisible straight stitches over the beaded area to make sure the beads sit snug to the fabric and are secure.

Finishing your work

Remove the hoop. Use a fine water spray to remove traces of water-soluble pen. Iron around the edges of the beaded motif or on the back. Wash gently by hand.

Beaded cardigan PROJECT

Seed beads in red and shades of green are transformed into two juicy-looking cherries that complement the gentle pink of this cardigan. While the beaded trim at the cuffs and hem is sewn directly onto the garment, the cherries and leaves are worked on a piece of pale pink organza, which is then fastened to the cardigan. This makes the embroidery easier to work and position. It also means you can easily stitch the motif to another garment later, should you wish.

YOU WILL NEED

- 18cm (7in) square of pale pink organza (or other finely woven, lightweight pale pink fabric)
- water-soluble pen
- embroidery hoop
- 10g (⅓oz) size 9 red seed beads
- 2g (⅛oz) size 9 emerald green seed beads
- 5g (¼oz) size 9 light green seed beads
- sewing needle
- red, green, and pink polyester sewing threads, to match the beads and cardigan
- fabric glue

- fine paintbrush
- scissors
- pale pink cardigan in a fine knit (lambswool, angora, and cashmere are all ideal)

1 Trace the cherry template on p.57 onto the organza using the water-soluble pen. Secure the fabric in the embroidery hoop. Outline the cherries with red beads, applying three beads at a time. Work two more rings of beads within the outline, then fill in the centre circles with a few short rows of beads. Secure the beads with safety stitches. Work a row of emerald green beads for the stalks. Work the outline of the leaves in light green beads and fill in with rows of beads.

2 Remove the embroidery from the hoop. Working on the underside of the organza, paint a thin line of fabric glue around the entire outside edge of the embroidery and leave it to dry.

3 Cut away the fabric around the edges of the embroidery so no fabric is visible from the front. Place the motif in position and secure it to the cardigan using small oversewing stitches around the edge and pink sewing thread to match the cardigan.

4 Using pink thread and two backstitches for each bead, secure red seed beads at 1.5cm (⅝in) intervals around the cuffs, just at the top of the ribbing. Work the thread from one bead to the next, using tiny running stitches. Do not pull the thread too tightly.

5 Work two more rows above the rows just worked. Space the beads for the second row between the beads of the first row. The beads in the third row should be exactly above the beads in the first. Work the same beaded border around the ribbing on the lower edge of the cardigan.

Templates

Shoe bag (pp.26-27)

Apron (pp.30-31)

Cardigan (pp.54-55)

Sarong (pp.34–35)

Tea towel (pp.38–39)

Enlarge by 110% on photocopier

Cushion cover (pp.42–43)

Appliqué throw (pp.50-51)

Enlarge by 120% on a photocopier

Index

The authors

A talented and dedicated team of crafters, all experts in their field, contributed towards the making of this book.

Fiona Goble

silkscreening

stencilling

appliqué

bead embroidery

Momtaz Begum-Hossain

fabric marbling

fabric painting

Susie Johns

dip-dyeing

tie-dyeing

block printing

Dorothy Wood

patchwork

Jane Cameron

batik

ACKNOWLEDGMENTS

Dorling Kindersley would like to thank Fiona Corbridge for her invaluable input in the early stages of development, Ira Sharma and Era Chawla for design assistance, Jane Ewart for photography art direction, Ruth Jenkinson for photography, Carly Churchill for hand-modelling and photographic assistance, Meryl Davies for photographic assistance, Hilary Mandleberg for sense-checking, Ria Holland for design assistance, Katie Hardwicke for proofreading, and Marie Lorimer for indexing.